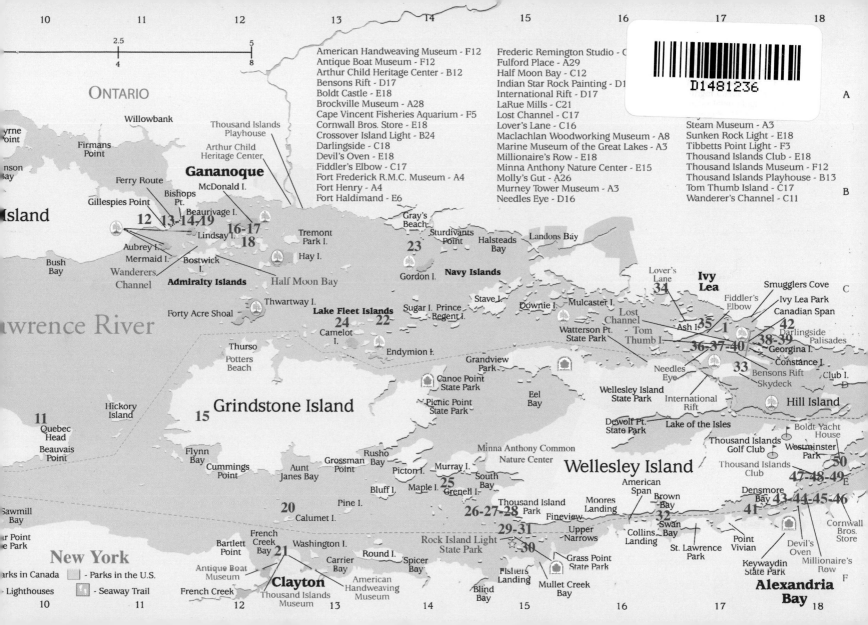

The Thousand Islands

Ian Coristine

Acknowledgements

This book would not exist were it not for the encouragement and support of a great many people. Joan Michie and Shane Sanford gave me the initial push to get the ball rolling several years ago. Dave Goulet's amazing aircraft design, the Challenger, has been instrumental in allowing me to share the privileged view from above. Paul Malo has not only provided encouragement, but generously shared his wealth of knowledge of the history of the place as well as his ideas. Dave O'Malley's fine graphics grace the cover. Michael Keyser helped create the original map that now serves three books. DxO Labs in Boulogne France, provided me with astonishing software that makes every image technically the best it can be, and Lyne Henderson took charge to ensure that the printing followed suit. Don McGowan pointed me in a new direction when he organized the first exhibition of my work at the Brockville Arts Center. The Antique Boat Museum has since taken his initiative a few steps further. My wife Mary and children Hayley and Scotty have helped in countless ways, especially for putting up with me when I get into tunnel vision mode on a project. There are so very many people along the river and elsewhere who have encouraged and supported my efforts that there is no way to mention them individually, but I hope each knows this work would not be the same without their valued contributions. My sincere thanks to all.

Prints of the images are available

The Thousand Islands serves as a catalogue as well as a book. For those who love the area and would enjoy decorating office, home or cottage with these or other Thousand Islands scenes, high resolution archival giclée art prints suitable for framing can be ordered from: www.1000islandsphotoart.com. If you wish to receive newsletters during the winter months that include images of the area to help with seasonal withdrawal, and for use as computer wallpaper, please add your name to the notification list you will find there.

Published by 1000 Islands Photo Art Inc. www.1000islandsphotoart.com   Copyright © Ian Coristine
Produced by Henderson Printing (Brockville, ON) www.hendersonprinting.com. Printed in Hong Kong.

Library and Archives Canada Cataloguing in Publication

Coristine, Ian, 1949-
The Thousand Islands : III / Ian Coristine.

ISBN 0-9730419-4-3

1. Thousand Islands (N.Y. and Ont.)--Aerial photographs.
2. Landscape photography-1000 Islands (N.Y. and Ont.)
I. Title.
FC3095.T43C673 2006   971.3'705'0222   C2006-900828-0

Also by the author:

Water, Wind and Sky

The 1000 Islands

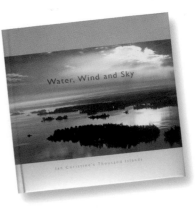

I never planned to do this book, nor the two that preceded it. Quite the contrary. After finishing my second book of photography of the Thousand Islands, I promised myself there would be no more.

No more getting up before the sun. No more freezing with the doors off the plane on cold fall mornings. No more setting off at dinner time to chase the last rays of sun in hopes of capturing that elusive image – only to return in the dark to face the accusing eyes of Molly, my Irish Setter, for having abandoned her yet again.

It was all unplanned and very unexpected. My business had been planes, not books. In 1992 I purchased a set of pontoons and figured that since I was now a "boat" owner, I should go exploring. So with a couple of friends, off we went, not caring where.

Ninety minutes later, I found myself looking down on one of the most beautiful and captivating places I had ever seen. It was a defining moment in my life. A quest began and three years later I found a little island, quite literally one in a thousand.

Storms, winds, raging water and rugged granite aren't exactly conducive to sheltering fragile airplanes. Amazingly, this island had a perfect natural harbor that included a sloping lawn so I could taxi onto land and tie down securely behind the cottage. It was offered for sale just once in the last century.

The photography wasn't planned either. It evolved from my enthusiasm to share this discovery with friends, to help them understand what wonders awaited. Unable to find photos or books that conveyed the magic, and finding myself living out on the river with a camera, boat and plane, I felt that if I didn't take advantage of this opportunity it might not present itself again.

I wanted a book that would provide a thorough overview of all that was here, not just random views. I wanted a map that would point out the elusive historical sites and also serve as a guide by revealing every photo's location. It would be the book I had been looking for, but couldn't find.

Apparently many others wanted the same, as it proved a surprising success. It gave me the courage to do a second quite different book, "Water, Wind and Sky", more a look at the raw beauty of the place than its most recognized views. When a fourth printing of the original book was needed, it occurred to me that the river is constantly flowing and changing and that the book should too. This then, unexpectedly, is the result.

Tibbetts Point Light has marked the eastern extremity of the Great Lakes and the entrance to the St. Lawrence since 1827. River pilots board ships at nearby Cape Vincent, to guide them through the confined channels and labyrinth of islands that follow.

Cape Vincent's strong French roots began when Samuel de Champlain visited in 1615. French missionaries followed and the area was later purchased by a French count who hoped to rescue Napoleon from his exile in St. Helena and make this his home.

Connected to the mainland and the City of Kingston via a short ferry ride, Wolfe Island and its village of Marysville is a world apart. At 54 square miles, Wolfe is the largest of the islands, traded to Canada for Niagara's Grande Isle in the 1822 Treaty of Ghent.

The largest fortification west of Quebec City is Fort Henry, originally built during the War of 1812 to protect the Royal Dockyards then located on the center peninsula, now the home of Royal Military College. Historic Kingston lies beyond.

Surprisingly, Fort Henry's armament wasn't aimed towards the water, but inland, down this carefully engineered slope to protect against land-based attack. The design's success is borne out by the fact that the main action seen here has been tobogganing.

Remington Typewriter's William O. Wyckoff was one of the first of many business barons to build a palatial summer home in the Thousand Islands. When Carlton Villa was finally completed in 1894, Wyckoff moved in to enjoy his first night. He never awoke.

In the 1920s, the 185-foot steamer *Schoolcraft* caught fire and was run ashore here near Quebec Head to save its crew of fourteen. Countless wrecks and very clear water has given the Thousand Islands a reputation for offering the world's finest freshwater diving.

At the foot of Howe, a transition begins from broad farming islands to small granite outcroppings, the high points of a Precambrian mountain range known as the Frontenac Arch that linked eastern Ontario's Canadian Shield with New York's Adirondacks.

In 1855, a lighthouse was built here on Red Horse Island, just off Bishops Point near Gananoque.
It was removed in 1968, making way for a more colorful landmark for passing boaters to enjoy.

The road hiccups here at the eastern tip of Howe, the third largest of the islands, where a cable ferry serves as the bridge to complete the connection, making this just one of four islands where residents can drive to their door.

I find it interesting that fog and mist will often cloak one part of the river such as here at Grindstone Island, while leaving the rest in the clear. I find myself drawn to the fog, despite the fact that it demands great care and respect when flying.

An increasing number of cruise ships visit the area, but only one actually lives here. The *Canadian Empress* drops anchor in the Admiralty Islands on its way to Quebec City to spend a night among a thousand islands and a million stars.

Not all islands are big enough to meet the requirements for building a cottage, but there are other ways to skin a cat. As a result, shoals here often command extraordinary prices.

It's not quite Venice, but perhaps the cottager's equivalent. Named after members of the British Admiralty, this group off Gananoque is the westernmost cluster of the distinctive granite and pine islands that make up much of the region.

Two boats trade wakes at sunset as they round the gap between Gillespie's Point and Bishop's Point at the eastern end of the Bateau Channel near Gananoque.

Calumet is a native term for peace pipe and a fitting choice for this island as it once served French Voyageurs as a "pipe stop", one of a series of regularly spaced resting sites to provide a break in their frantic seasonal rush to and from distant fur trapping regions.

George Boldt's 6500 square foot houseboat *La Duchesse* boasted ten bedrooms, five baths, two fireplaces and a dancing deck. Rescued and restored from sinking to serve as a cottage for many years, it now can be toured at Clayton's Antique Boat Museum.

The Lake Fleet Group lies along the border in a peaceful three-mile stretch of river, just off Grindstone Island's north shore. Two islands, Endymion and Camelot belong to the St. Lawrence Islands National Park and offer boaters pristine mooring sites.

Cormorants are one of several species to have made a prolific comeback on the river. Local fishermen see them as competitors and don't look upon them fondly, but their return is a very welcome sign of improvement in the environment.

The Lake Fleet Islands carry the names of ships of the British fleet that served on the Great Lakes in the War of 1812. Their beauty and tranquility is in complete contrast to the names several carry, like Bloodletter, Scorpion, Axeman and Deathdealer.

"Woodies" are a favored mode of transportation and recreation in the Thousand Islands. This one was built at the Hutchinson Boat Works in Alexandria Bay in 1931 and still graces the river as part of the Antique Boat Museum's "in water" fleet.

A visit to Thousand Island Park, founded as a Methodist campground in 1875, is to take a step back in time to a delightful gingerbread fairyland with a tight-knit community of families, some of whom have been coming here for seven generations.

Tender loving care is an important ingredient in maintaining the historic charm, but far more than a museum village, T.I. Park remains an active and lively summer community that reunites families and friends who unfailingly return from across the nation.

With hundreds of cottages built away from the shoreline in the village of T.I. Park, boathouses become very highly prized.

Decommissioned in 1958 after one hundred and eleven years of service, Rock Island Light now serves as a state park picnic area, offering a wonderful vantage point for viewing ships as they pass in the adjacent St. Lawrence Seaway shipping channel.

"Yachts" in the Thousand Islands come in all shapes and sizes, some of them a little too wide to fit in a boathouse.

Having served his jail sentence following a career of pirating which included robbing, burning and sinking the steamship *Sir Robert Peel* here in 1838, Bill Johnston returned to the scene of his crime to become the keeper of Rock Island Light in 1853.

Guess who's coming to dinner? Ships thread their way through narrow confines in the 1000 Islands, often very close to cottages, but not usually this close. After losing its steering, this "laker" ran aground at St. Helena Island just east of the U.S. Span.

The 1000 Islands are best viewed from above, where the next shoreline isn't hiding the view beyond. I'm accustomed to the privileged aerial perspective, but not to the total peace and quiet that accompanied it on my first visit to the top of the Skydeck.

Boats are fundamental to the Thousand Islands, as are marinas. Islanders depend on both to get home. My wife says she'd be happier with island life if there were a bridge to shore. For most islanders, myself included, a bridge would spoil everything.

It's all in the details. This boathouse was in a sad state of repair when I happened to strike up a conversation with its new owner, whose summer job it had been to paint, decades before. He has since repeated the job, no doubt with considerably more care.

Dashwood Island brings with it a significant problem.
It offers an overwhelming number of compelling spots to relax and enjoy the view.

One option is to use the porch for morning coffee as the sun rises above Tom Thumb and Hill Islands, and at the end of the day retire to the gazebo to watch it set behind Wood and Ash Islands.

The Canadian Span provides 120 feet of clearance over the Canadian Channel, far more than actually needed. The height provided options for the St. Lawrence Seaway, which was still only a concept when the U.S. and Canadian bridges were designed.

Canada's portion of the 1000 Islands Bridge System consists of three elegant sections which carry traffic from the mainland to Hill Island, where a mile up the road a short and easily missed masonry bridge spans a tiny gap over the International Rift to the U.S.

On August 14, 1760, the British warship *H.M.S. Onondaga* lowered a boat here in pursuit of French and Indian attackers. Later, when the ship's crew could find neither the boat nor the men, they named this "The Lost Channel."

Location, location, location. The quest to own a cottage on "Millionaire's Row" in the late 1800s went to great lengths. To build this cottage at Longue Vue with its stone boathouse and clock tower, a shoal first had to be transformed into an island.

In 1843, Thomas Darling built Darlingside, which he operated as a general store and cordwood depot supplying steamships on the river. He traded shop credit to local farmers in return for their wood and built himself a prosperous business out of the wilderness.

George Pullman (of Pullman railroad car fame) invited President Ulysses S. Grant and fellow Civil War Generals, Sherman and Sheridan to his island in 1872. The press wrote glowing reports of the area, initiating a popularity that continues to this day.

For over a century, an elegant footbridge at the foot of Cherry Island has framed ships of all shapes and sizes passing alongside in the St. Lawrence Seaway shipping channel.

Cherry Island's Belora is the surviving cottage of a pair, built in the late 1800s by philanthropist Nathan Strauss and his business partner, Abraham Abraham. Strauss' fortune came from Macy's in New York City, then the world's largest department store.

Alexandria Bay was once a backwater servicing the timber trade, but when the business tycoons of the Northeast's major cities discovered the magnificence of the area in the late 1800s, it was transformed into one of the premiere resorts on the continent.

To most, construction of any of these buildings would represent the major project of a lifetime. To George Boldt, they were just a portion of what he built here, all secondary to his primary focus, New York City's Waldorf Astoria.

An unfinished dream, George Boldt's magnificent castle and Heart Island complex was intended as a gift for his wife Louise. Devastated by her unexpected death in 1904, he immediately halted construction and never again set foot on the island.

Rising ninety feet above the water, a clock and chimes tower crowned Boldt Castle's powerhouse, but it never saw use beyond serving as a residence for a caretaker whose job it was to chase away the curious after construction was halted.

George Boldt's Yacht House housed a fleet of some sixty boats including his 104-foot houseboat, *La Duchesse*, the 102-foot steam and sailing yacht *Louise*, plus racing, pleasure and utility boats, several of which remain here on display.

When Sunken Rock Light was built in 1847, its light and the others on the river were fueled by sperm whale oil, but the international slaughter of whales was so great that by 1860, lighthouses were forced to switch to kerosene.

Sleepy now, but when the tiny village of Rockport wakes up, so does the activity. The village serves as an embarkation point for tour and dive boats, is home to a busy marina, and offers a delightful setting for a pair of popular restaurants.

With the river's currents beneath, crossing the ice has always been a life-threatening gamble until a local cottage industry began producing iceboats. They not only solve the transportation problem, but also offer a new and entertaining form of winter recreation.

Former owners of Estrellita felt that their delightful setting deserved more glass, so installed an enormous picture window to let in the view. Subsequent owners found themselves sharing their meals with passing boaters. The window has since been replaced.

Zavikon Island is known to millions as having the world's shortest international bridge, providing access from the cottage in Canada to its backyard in the United States.

When prominent businessmen from the Northeast's major cities built cottages here, they typically employed the finest architects of the time. Sunnyside's also designed New York City's Waldorf, the Plaza and Dakota buildings as well as Montreal's Windsor Hotel.

One of the appealing aspects of the Thousand Islands is that it offers many uniquely different neighborhoods that don't necessarily follow the traditional form of a village. This one is known as the Summerland Group.

The river is now laying claim to Ina Island's boathouse, but it once stood proudly, hosting major events for local society in its upstairs ballroom. Later, Ina earned a somewhat different reputation when it served as a brothel.

Thanks in part to preservation groups who erected nesting platforms in the islands, Osprey numbers have surged. One evening while flying low along a shoreline, I was astounded when one leapt from its nest to charge me!

Easily seen from above, but much more difficult to spot from a boat, countless shoals lie in wait for the unwary.
The problem is aggravated by a seasonal variation in water levels of some four feet, so the threat is constantly changing.

While much of Grenadier Island is privately owned by cottagers, four separate portions offer docking and camping, all part of the St. Lawrence Islands National Park. They are connected by this delightful nature trail, which is like walking into a painting.

In the 1990s, a ship emptied its ballast tanks in Lake Superior inadvertently introducing the zebra mussel, which quickly proliferated. Initially seen as a threat, they have proven a boon to swimmers, filtering the water to a clarity not seen in decades.

I saw this "photo op" developing while the ship was still miles away, so landed and waited to save fuel before restarting and popping up to capture this colorful view of Three Sisters Lighthouse.

Islands here were not always greatly valued. The story goes that in 1791 Grenadier Island was purchased for four pots of rum, and later the owner would have been glad to trade it back for a beaver pelt. Golfers and residents now value it somewhat differently

Summer residents have been coming to Grenadier Island for some time. Archaeologists have unearthed artifacts from a seasonal native encampment on adjacent Squaw Island that date back 7,000 years.

Frederick Bourne, the wealthiest of the 1000 Islands establishment, built Singer Sewing Machine into the first global corporation. His family thought he had built a small hunting lodge until they rounded Chippewa Bay's Cedar Island for their first visit.

Ernest Flagg modeled "The Towers" after an English Castle, "Woodstock", complete with dungeons and secret passageways, including this one that allowed servants to discretely monitor guests' needs. Flagg also designed New York City's Chrysler building.

Ships from around the world pass within a stone's throw of Singer Castle. When their sewing machines were slow sellers at $42 each, Singer's Frederick Bourne conceived a revolutionary purchase plan of one dollar per week that made him a fortune.

Only the chimney remains from a War of 1812 blockhouse situated here on Chimney Island at the edge of the Canadian channel. Rebuilt by an historically minded owner, it overlooks a somewhat more ambitious project, Dark Island's Singer Castle.

Most common when the temperature drops in the fall, sea smoke is formed when the warmth rising from the water meets much cooler air, frequently creating mystical and sometimes haunting scenes while also making navigation a challenge.

Chippewa Bay has always been favored by those who prefer to keep a lower profile. Amongst its prominent former residents was artist Frederic Remington who owned a nearby island. His work and career are honored at a noteworthy museum in Ogdensburg.

Many islanders consider themselves privileged stewards of irreplaceable properties. Future generations will take pleasure in this magnificent Wyanoke Island boathouse built in the 1890s by shipbuilder and New York Yacht Club Commodore C.B. Orcutt.

"The River" was named when Jacques Cartier sailed into it in 1535 on the anniversary of the St. Lawrence's death, while searching for a route to China. His progress was stopped by rapids about a hundred miles downstream, a place he named La Chine.

Islanders delight in footbridges of every size and description. This one at Algonquin Lodge near Jones Creek was built by Sir Clifford Sifton, whose efforts to promote and encourage immigration played a major role in settling and developing Canada's west.

In 2002, UNESCO designated the 1000 Islands as an International Biosphere Reserve, recognizing it as a unique habitat for a wide variety of plant and animal life, some quite rare. Jones Creek, with its pristine and extensive wetland area is an important element.

If a quiet day is suddenly interrupted by a major uproar from the local bird population, it is almost certainly because a mink is on the prowl. Very secretive, I'd never have spotted this one without the general outcry.

I find snakes fascinating, but neither my wife nor my dog share my interest. When my Irish Setter unexpectedly came across this tiny grass snake, she jumped two feet, straight up. A pretty good effort, but only about half as high as my wife would have managed.

Jones Creek was once a busy waterway with significant boat traffic servicing two gristmills, a lumber mill and the hamlet of Yonge Mills. When a bridge was first built across it in 1904 to allow access to Brockville, angry locals promptly blew it up.

I often enjoy a morning row up Jones Creek with my camera close at hand. The peace and tranquility of these outings allows me to see the world quite differently than when I'm looking down at it from above.

The elderly couple who previously owned our island told me it was "a green leaf place", and while green, there would be no place I'd rather be, but when the leaves and temperature fell, it was time to go. Truer words were never spoken.

Most thunderstorms are convective, being fed by warm air rising from heated land. The cooler river dampens convection, so thunderstorms typically drift down either shoreline, offering islanders a grandstand seat in the clear. Not so with this one.

Mother Goose chose our island for her nest, which she sat on faithfully, even coming to trust my dog and me, while father stayed close but was not quite so trusting. Sadly, it was all in vain as one morning she was gone, leaving behind a nest of un-hatched eggs

This family fared better, but was not quite so trusting. In an effort to keep clear of me, they steered their brood a little too close to a red wing blackbird's nest. She dive bombed them mercilessly until they moved away.

Some say that to qualify as an island, it must be above water year round and have at least one tree. Others insist on two. Either way, the seagulls and cormorants have claimed this one in the Amateur Islands as home.

Built in 1848, Crossover Island Light marks a series of dangerous shoals at a turning point in the St. Lawrence Seaway shipping channel where it crosses over from the American to the Canadian side of the river.

Weather plays a major role in island life, particularly on a small one. While a big blow or storm may mean having to postpone or even cancel a trip to shore, the 360-degree vistas mean you'll never miss a glorious moment.

"Woodies" have their charms, but being antiques, they require considerable upkeep, and not just sanding and varnish. This one met its demise because of a fuel leak, encouraging its passengers into an impromptu swim.

St. Lawrence Union Campground was the first Canadian Park, established in 1875 by the Methodists. Like T.I. Park, the tents soon gave way to cottages and a more permanent community, initially named Union Park, now known as Butternut Bay.

On June 26th, 1930, the residents here at McDonald Point were witnesses to an enormous explosion.
Carrying a cargo of dynamite, the *J. B. King* was struck by lightning a few hundred feet across the Brockville Narrows.

I spent considerable time climbing and surfing this ship's bow wave trying to capture a unique perspective. Initially, I wasn't noticed but when I was, the helmsman and his foghorn woke up most of Brockville in voicing his displeasure.

A full moon rising over the river is always a special event. When it is accompanied by a haunting serenade from a quartet of loons and backed by the chorus from a gaggle of geese, it is magic.

One of Brockville's charms is that it offers the potential for a pastoral lifestyle while living right in the downtown core.

Less celebrated than its neighbor Fulford Place, but arguably even more photogenic, Thornton Cliff brings the style of the grand country homes of England to the cliffs at the east end of Brockville.

This shot cost me a lens shade, as it went overboard in the scramble to catch this sleepy pair while still on one leg. It joins a growing number of lens caps, filters and other paraphernalia that I've donated to the river.

Once known as "Snarlingtown" because of bickering over its future name, Brockville eventually took its name from Sir Isaac Brock, "the man who saved Canada" in the War of 1812. He died in action, leading his men to victory at Queenston Heights.

Were you to ask a Thousand Islander why this magical place means so much to them, there would be a thousand answers. This is just one of them.

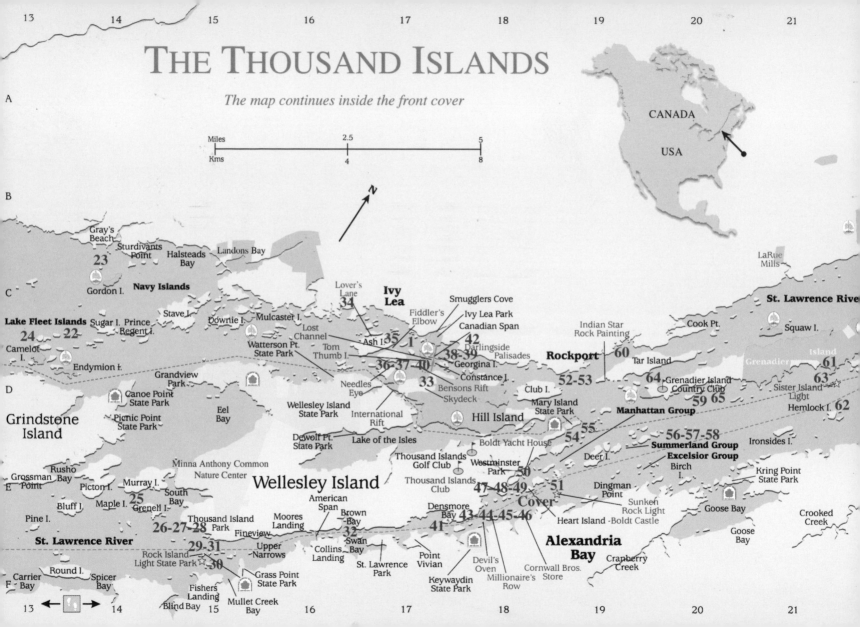

THE THOUSAND ISLANDS

The map continues inside the front cover

CANADA

USA

Miles | 2.5 | 5
Kms | 4 | 8

N

A

B

C

D

E

F

Gray's Beach
Sturdivants Point
Halsteads Bay
Landons Bay
23
Gordon I. **Navy Islands**
Stave I.

Lover's Lane
34 **Ivy Lea**
Smugglers Cove
Fiddler's Elbow
Ivy Lea Park
Canadian Span

LaRue Mills

St. Lawrence River

Indian Star Rock Painting
Cook Pt.
Squaw I.

Lake Fleet Islands
24 22 Sugar I. Prince Regent I.
Camelot I.
Downie I. Mulcaster I.
Lost Channel
Watterson Pt. State Park
Tom Thumb I.
Ash I.
35 1
38-39
Darlingside Palisades
42
Georgina I.
Constance I.

Rockport
60 Tar Island

64 Grenadier Island Country Club
59 65

Island
Grenadier
61
63
Sister Island Light
Hemlock I. 62

Endymion I.
Grandview Park
Needles Eye
36-37-40
33
Bensons Rift
Skydeck
52-53
Club I.

Canoe Point State Park
Eel Bay
Wellesley Island State Park
International Rift
Mary Island State Park

Manhattan Group

Grindstone Island
Picnic Point State Park
Dewolf Pt. State Park
Lake of the Isles
Hill Island
Boldt Yacht House
54 55
Deer I.
Summerland Group
Excelsior Group
Ironsides I.
Birch I.
Kring Point State Park

Grossman Bay
Rusho Point
Minna Anthony Common Nature Center
Thousand Islands Golf Club
Westminster Park
50
Dingman Point
Goose Bay

Picton I. Murray I.
South Bay
Wellesley Island
Thousand Islands Club
47-48-49
51
Sunken Rock Light
Heart Island - Boldt Castle

Bluff I. Maple I.
25 Grenell I.
American Span
Brown Bay
Densmore Bay
Cover
43-44-45-46
Cornwall Bros. Store
Goose Bay

Pine I.
26-27-28
Thousand Island Park
Moores Landing
Fineview
32
Swan Bay
41
Alexandria Bay
Cranberry Creek
Crooked Creek

St. Lawrence River
29-31
Rock Island Light State Park
30
Upper Narrows
Collins Landing
St. Lawrence Park
Point Vivian
Devil's Oven
Millionaire's Row

Carrier Bay
Round I.
Spicer Bay
Fishers Landing
Mullet Creek Bay
Grass Point State Park
Keywaydin State Park

Blind Bay